DATE DUE

Drug Abuse and Society™

METHAMPHETAMINE
The Dangers of Crystal Meth

The Rosen Publishing Group, Inc., New York

Frank Spalding

For George

Published in 2007 by The Rosen Publishing Group, Inc.
29 East 21st Street, New York, NY 10010

First Edition

Library of Congress Cataloging-in-Publication Data

Spalding, Frank.
Methamphetamine: the dangers of crystal meth/
by Frank Spalding.—1st ed.
    p. cm.—(Drug abuse and society)
Includes bibliographical references.
ISBN-13: 978-1-4042-0912-1
ISBN-10: 1-4042-0912-3 (library binding)
1. Methamphetamine abuse—Social aspects.
2. Methamphetamine—Social aspects.
I. Title. II. Series.
RC568.A45S63 2007
362.29'9—dc22
                                                        2006008489

Manufactured in the United States of America

Contents

INTRODUCTION

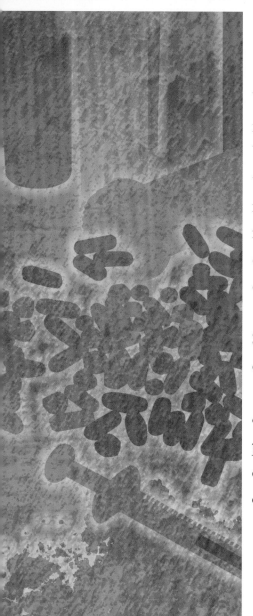

Methamphetamine, commonly known as meth, is one of the most popular illicit drugs in the United States. It is simple to make, profitable for dealers, and highly addictive. Unlike drugs that must be smuggled across the globe to reach North America, meth is manufactured in clandestine laboratories, or meth labs. Many of the ingredients used to create meth can be purchased over the counter at a drugstore. In 2003, more than 10,000 meth labs were seized in the United States. That's an average of 200 meth labs in each state.

Meth can be swallowed, snorted, smoked, or injected directly into a user's veins. A person using meth feels an initial rush of euphoria, or intense pleasure. The effects of the drug can last for a very long time,

Meth can come in solid chunks or in powder form, as seen here. The color of meth can vary depending on the ingredients used to make it.

sometimes up to twelve hours. During this time, users' body temperatures rise and their heart rates increase. They experience increased wakefulness and energy, and their appetites decrease.

All illicit drugs take a toll on those who use them, but meth is especially damaging. Once meth's initial rush wears off, the user often feels intense depression, coupled with a strong desire to consume more of the drug. Some meth users go into violent rages, making them dangerous to themselves and to others. Chronic long-term use of methamphetamine can result in paranoia, hallucinations, convulsions, heart attack, brain damage, stroke, and eventually death. Even if meth users know they are becoming addicts, they are often powerless to stop their downward spiral.

The U.S. government has passed a number of different laws intended to curb meth use. These laws don't just punish meth users—they make it more difficult to acquire the raw chemical materials used to manufacture the drug. With any luck, legislation will help discourage dealers from creating the drug and stop potential users from trying it. However, laws alone will never be able to keep people from using meth. Education is the key to helping potential users decide to stay away from methamphetamine.

CHAPTER 1

Meth: An Addictive Stimulant

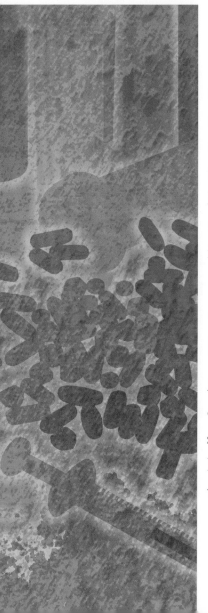

Methamphetamine is a stimulant, or a drug that increases the activity of the body's nervous system. Stimulants act on a person's central nervous system, making a user feel more energetic, alert, and productive. Some stimulants, such as caffeine, are perfectly legal. Other stimulants, such as cocaine, crack, ecstasy, and methamphetamine, are illegal.

THE HISTORY OF METHAMPHETAMINE

Methamphetamine is chemically similar to a drug called amphetamine, which was first synthesized in 1887 by a German chemist. In the 1920s, researchers experimented with using amphetamines to treat a number of

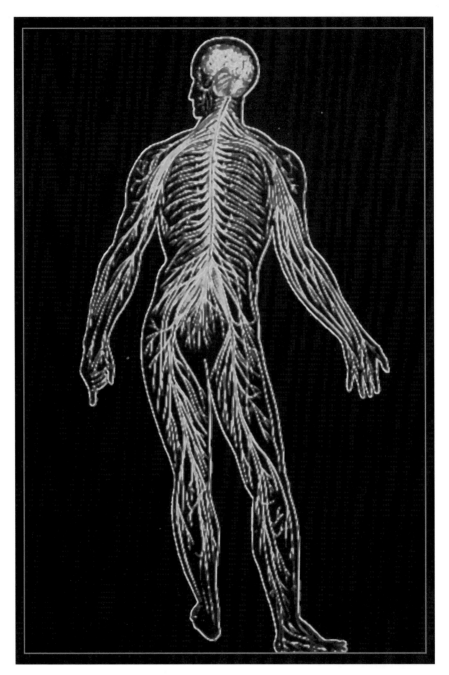

This digitized image shows the nervous system, which includes the brain, the spinal cord, and various nerves and receptors throughout the body. Some doctors think that meth may cause irreversible damage to the nervous system, which is the body's main communication center.

diseases, such as epilepsy, schizophrenia, and alcoholism. The drug was also suggested as a treatment for depression.

By 1927, scientists and doctors discovered that amphetamine raised patients' blood pressure and enlarged their nasal passages. It also expanded their bronchial passages, the tubes that carry air in and out of the lungs when a person breathes. A variation of amphetamine was first commercially released as a decongestant under the name Benzedrine in 1928.

Benzedrine could be purchased at most local pharmacies with a prescription. The drug came in inhalers similar to the kind used by asthmatics. Many people who used Benzedrine discovered that it had a mild euphoric effect. It wasn't long before people hit upon the idea of breaking open the inhaler to consume the drug all at once. Inside the inhaler, a small strip of paper soaked in the drug could be removed and swallowed.

Slowly but surely, Benzedrine grew in popularity. By the time reports emerged about the spread of Benzedrine inhaler misuse, people all over the country were using the drug.

By the late 1930s, amphetamine was being manufactured in pill form, further increasing the availability of the drug. The pill form of amphetamine was intended to combat narcolepsy, a disease in which sufferers fall asleep at unpredictable times.

Methamphetamine, which is a chemical related to amphetamine, was synthesized by a Japanese chemist in 1919. It had a very similar effect to amphetamine, with two important distinctions: methamphetamine was much more potent and much cheaper to make. It didn't become widely available until 1942, when the Second World War was under way.

METH AND WAR

During World War II (1939–1945), methamphetamine was distributed to soldiers on both sides of the conflict. Pilots often took to the air with a supply of methamphetamine to help them stay alert during long missions. The Axis powers of Germany and Japan gave methamphetamine to their soldiers to help them stay awake and energized in combat. Methamphetamine allowed soldiers to perform better with less rest than they could otherwise. Many soldiers fighting for the Allied powers, such as Great Britain, Canada, and the United States, also used methamphetamine on the battlefield.

By the time the Axis powers surrendered in 1945, World War II had spread tremendous destruction across the world. Millions of people lost their lives, and many cities had been reduced to rubble. Some countries took a long time to rebuild completely. Amid all this ruin and chaos, almost no one noticed that in Japan, meth addiction was spreading throughout the population.

POSTWAR ADDICTION

One of the conditions of Japan's surrender after World War II was that it virtually dismantle its military. Without a standing military,

Japan no longer had a need for methamphetamine, and it was immediately banned.

However, there was still a lot of the drug in storage. Many of the soldiers who had grown accustomed to using it did not want to stop after the war was over. Organized crime syndicates realized that these addicts presented a huge potential customer base. Even though methamphetamine was banned, it became widely available on the black market.

These U.S. fighter planes fly over rural Italy in 1942. Active combat can be physically and mentally exhausting for soldiers. During World War II, some pilots and infantrymen were given methamphetamine to remain energetic and alert during battle.

Many American servicemen returned from fighting in World War II, and later, from the Korean War (1950–1953), with a desire to get more methamphetamine. It was still possible to buy Benzedrine and other types of amphetamine and methamphetamine with a prescription, but soon this wasn't enough to keep up with user demand. Whatever the intended medical uses of amphetamine and methamphetamine, it was clear that more and more people were acquiring them for recreational use. By the 1950s, doctors had grown concerned about excessively prescribing Benzedrine to their patients. In response to spreading stimulant abuse in the United States, the U.S. Drug Abuse Regulation and Control Act of 1970 made amphetamine illegal.

ILLEGAL CHEMISTRY

With powerful stimulants now restricted by law, drug dealers learned how to make meth in illegal laboratories. During the 1960s, the manufacture of meth was largely controlled by outlaw motorcycle gangs.

By the 1970s, cocaine became widely available. This made it the stimulant of choice among drug users, and methamphetamine became less common. Although it was not as widespread as before, meth did not disappear. By the 1980s, new ways to make meth were discovered that were fairly simple. Although yielding a much less pure form of the drug, meth manufacturing became easy and inexpensive. As the cost of the drug went down, its popularity began to rise once more.

Meth is now viewed as one of the most dangerous drugs in the United States. It was once considered a drug that mainly appealed to low-income white men living in rural areas. Although meth is still popular with this group, today all sorts of people use methamphetamine.

MYTHS AND FACTS

Myth: Using meth gives you energy and helps you lose weight.

Fact: Because it increases metabolism and suppresses the appetite, meth does cause weight loss—extreme weight loss. Food gives people stamina in the form of calories that can be burned for energy. Meth, however, burns through the body's natural stores of energy. After that energy is gone, the user crashes, sometimes sleeping for days at a time.

Myth: If a person does meth even once, he or she becomes a meth addict.

Fact: Although methamphetamine is a very addictive drug, some people use it without becoming addicts. There is no way to tell who will and who won't become an addict.

Myth: It's safe to use meth occasionally.

Fact: Meth is extremely toxic, and any amount may damage your body. Even if a person uses meth only once, he or she could still overdose on the drug, suffer a heart attack, or have a stroke.

ENHANCING PERFORMANCE

Many of the first amphetamine and methamphetamine addicts were those who initially took the drugs for other purposes, such as to stay awake or control their diet. Today, some people still use meth to get through commonplace tasks. They might use meth before a long shift at work, or during an all-night study session. According to Quest Diagnostics, a company that performs drug tests for employers and businesses, there was a 68 percent rise in the number of employees who tested positive for methamphetamine in the United States in 2004.

The Health and Human Services 2003 National Survey on Drug Use and Health found that 77 percent of drug abusers age eighteen and older had jobs. Many who are under the influence of meth during work just think that they're being productive, which is why the drug is becoming more popular among people in competitive and stressful lines of work. For instance, the California Bar Association has reported that one in four lawyers who seeks treatment for drug addiction is a habitual meth user. Even though these meth users may have what appear to be normal lives, they are still harming themselves.

When people turn to meth to help them meet their deadlines and work long hours, they push their bodies to the limits of their endurance. However, meth isn't a drug like caffeine. While it may increase wakefulness, too much meth will disrupt the central nervous system, making it difficult for a user to think clearly. College students who use meth or other illegal stimulants in an effort to finish writing term papers may complete their work, only to find the next day that it is nonsensical. In some industries, such as construction or farming, this disorientation can lead to workplace injuries.

CHAPTER 2

Users and Pushers

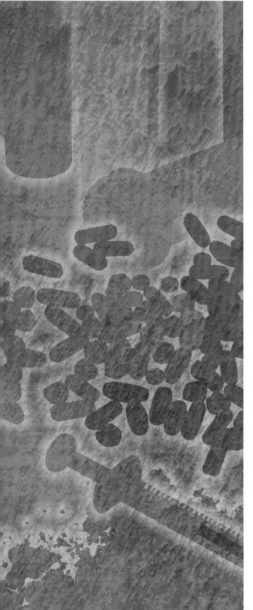

Meth can be swallowed, snorted, smoked, or dissolved in water and injected. Users who smoke or inject the drug experience an intense surge of pleasure, called a "rush" or "flash," soon after taking it. This rush generally occurs within just five to twenty minutes, and gradually fades away.

Meth's most significant effect, however, is the extreme amount of energy and wakefulness that the user experiences. The effects of meth last for a long time, anywhere from four to twelve hours. The intense high is one of the main reasons meth users like taking the drug so much. It is also one of the reasons people can become addicted so quickly. Few other drugs have such an intense and long-lasting effect on users. Then again, few drugs cause as much harm to users as meth.

This chemical solution, which was found in an illegal lab in Brazoria County in Texas, tested positive as meth. Before police raided the lab, crystal meth was being formed in the solution.

LOSING CONTROL

Lasting only a few minutes, the initial rush often becomes more elusive for meth users as their bodies build up tolerance for the drug. Users sometimes find themselves using meth over an entire weekend, staying awake the whole time, and trying to relive that initial rush. The longer meth users stay awake, the more out of control they become. They often grow confused, irritable, and extremely paranoid. Some begin to have minor hallucinations.

Repeatedly taking meth can keep users from sleeping for well over a week. They often keep consuming more of the drug to try to stay awake, but they are unable to recapture the euphoric effects of the first hit. This stage of meth use is known as tweaking. While tweaking, the user is likely to engage in simple, repetitive tasks. These tasks can include taking something apart and then putting it back together again, or repeatedly cleaning his or her room.

It's not uncommon for meth users to pick at the skin of their arms and face while tweaking, or hallucinate that there are insects (sometimes referred to as crank bugs) underneath their skin. At this point, their judgment is severely impaired, and there is an increased chance that they may harm themselves or others.

Even though chronic meth users can stay awake for days at a time, no one can stay awake forever. Eventually, users will give in to fatigue and depression. After staying awake for several days, meth users will crash, their body and brain completely exhausted. Users may sleep for several days straight following a meth binge.

When people try meth, they usually don't think they're going to become addicted. They often start using meth recreationally at social gatherings. Before long, they begin using it alone. As time passes, they find that they are unable to stop. Many start using meth by snorting it. They then progress to smoking it. At last, they start injecting it directly into their veins. Methamphetamine is so addictive, it can become more important than the user's job, friends, and loved ones. It can destroy the user's professional, social, and family life, and finally destroy his or her mind and body.

DRUG CARTELS

Mexican drug cartels control a good portion of the meth trade in the United States, though most of the meth in the United States is supplied by clandestine labs in California and Mexico. Many of these drug cartels were originally distributing South American cocaine. In the 1990s, they discovered that it was more profitable to manufacture and sell meth.

There are several reasons why drug cartels play such a dominant role in meth production. These cartels are well organized, well funded, and well connected. They also have one other important advantage—the ability to acquire ephedrine and pseudoephedrine easily.

These substances are crucial to the manufacture of meth, and their sale is restricted in many American states. In Mexico, however, even with restrictions on ephedrine and pseudoephedrine, dealers are still able to purchase the ingredients in bulk, allowing them to produce meth on a very large scale. The meth is then distributed throughout the United States by drug dealers. Meth abuse is most prevalent on the West Coast and in the Southwest and Midwest, but its popularity is spreading to the Northeast, Mexico, and Canada.

METH LABS

Most of today's meth is made in illegal labs. Pure methamphetamine has no color. Meth produced in illegal laboratories may be white, yellow, or come in darker colors, depending on what chemicals were used to make it. Meth can come in a granulated powder or be formed into solid chunks. The drug is often called by a number of different names, such as speed, crank, or Tina. Meth that comes in solid chunks is often called crystal, ice, or glass. These forms of the drug are also smokable.

Meth labs come in all sizes. Larger ones, known as super-labs, can take up an entire building. Superlabs produce large amounts of meth for distribution throughout the country. To be classified as a superlab, the laboratory must produce more than 10 pounds (4.5 kilograms) of meth within twenty-four hours. About 80 percent of all meth in the United States is produced in superlabs.

By the 1980s, most meth made in the United States was being manufactured in California. Although the West Coast is still the center of meth production in the United States, there are now illegal labs all across the country.

Many meth labs are set up in private homes. People who invest a few hundred dollars in ingredients can make their own meth. The fact that a good number of people who try to produce meth end up in jail, the hospital, or dead doesn't seem to deter would-be dealers.

INSIDE A METH LAB

Meth is a dangerous drug, but manufacturing it can be even more dangerous. Recipes for making meth have changed over the years, depending on the cost and availability of ingredients. One of the major ingredients in meth used to be a chemical called phenyl-2-propanone, which became a federally controlled substance in 1980. After this chemical was banned, meth was

The chemicals used to make meth can be extremely combustible. This well-equipped Texas meth lab shows some of the equipment used to manufacture the drug.

21

Ephedrine, Pseudoephedrine, and Phenylephrine

Ephedrine is a substance that is derived from certain plants. It has been used by various cultures for medicinal purposes. For instance, the Chinese herb ma huang contains ephedrine and is traditionally used to treat respiratory conditions such as asthma and bronchitis. Today, ephedrine and pseudoephedrine are used in cold medications. Pseudoephedrine is chemically similar to ephedrine but has less of a stimulative effect on the central nervous system.

Phenylephrine, a drug similar to ephedrine and pseudoephedrine, has recently been used as the active ingredient in decongestants. The adaptation of phenylephrine for use as a decongestant came after the United States began passing laws restricting the sale of pseudoephedrine. Although phenylephrine is considered to be a less effective decongestant than ephedrine and pseudoephedrine, it cannot be used to manufacture methamphetamine.

generally made from ephedrine and pseudoephedrine. The meth cooks who resorted to using ephedrine after they could no longer use phenyl-2-propanone found that ephedrine made the drug much more potent. Ephedrine and pseudoephedrine are primarily used in decongestants and can be found in many over-the-counter medicines. These medicines are combined with a number of other chemicals in a complicated and dangerous process that eventually yields illegal methamphetamine.

The other ingredients used to make meth are considerably more dangerous than nasal decongestants. These acidic substances

CAPTURADO

JOSE DE JESUS AMEZCUA CONTRERAS

In June 1998, police arrested Jose de Jesus Amezcua-Contreras.
Amezcua-Contreras was a leader of one of the most powerful Mexican
drug cartels that manufactured and sold meth. Amezcua-Contreras is now
serving a sentence in Mexico.

are strong enough to eat through skin and bone. They can include
chemicals found in drain cleaners and paint thinners, ammonia,
and sulfuric acid. Many of these chemicals are so toxic that even
being in a meth lab is dangerous. Some meth cooks suffer respiratory problems, nausea, dizziness, and disorientation from exposure
to these chemicals. Others are severely mutilated or even killed
when flammable substances in the labs catch fire or explode.

CHAPTER 3

Human Behavior and Drug Addiction

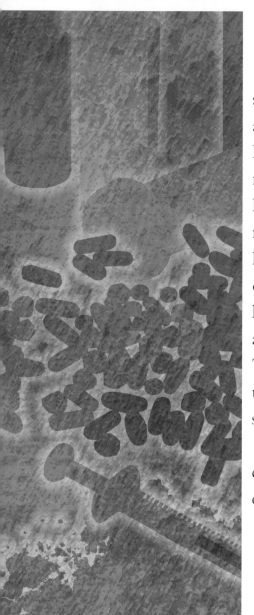

Methamphetamine has profound effects on the body. It dries out the skin and causes rashes, extensive sweating, insomnia, and diarrhea. It affects the part of the brain that regulates heart rate, body temperature, appetite, and mood. When someone takes meth, his or her heart rate increases, body temperature rises, and mood improves. This can place a heavy strain on the body and, over time, can result in damage to the heart and lungs. Meth users may experience cardiac arrhythmia, or an irregular heartbeat. Taking too much of the drug can cause a user to suffer convulsions, a heart attack, stroke, or death.

One very visible effect of the drug is the damage it does to a user's teeth. Meth often causes people to grind their teeth. It also dries out users' mouths and sometimes makes them crave sugary drinks. "Meth mouth" is a term used to describe the excessive tooth decay from which heavy meth users tend to suffer.

DISEASE

One of the biggest risks meth users face is the chance that they will contract a disease from other users. Meth is often smoked out of glass pipes. Users sharing hot pipes run the risk of getting burns and sores to the lips, mouth, or gums. They also face the danger of catching diseases such as human immunodeficiency virus (HIV) and hepatitis C, both of which are contracted through blood-to-blood contact. Sharing straws in order to snort the drug also puts users at risk of getting HIV and hepatitis C, a disease that attacks the liver and for which there is no cure. Sharing needles is the most dangerous way to take meth because HIV can be contracted through bodily fluids. If a person who is HIV-infected shares needles, there is a great chance that he or she is spreading the virus that causes acquired immunodeficiency syndrome (AIDS).

A link has also been made between a spike in HIV infections and people who have used meth as a party drug, according to the *San Francisco Chronicle*. Meth lowers users' inhibitions, increases their sex drive, and impairs their judgment. This may encourage them to engage in unsafe sex, dramatically increasing their risk for contracting HIV and other sexually transmitted diseases.

DON'T LET DRUG DEALERS CHANGE
THE FACE OF YOUR NEIGHBOURHOOD.
Call Crimestoppers anonymously on 0800 555 111.

METROPOLITAN POLICE *Working for a safer London*

This poster illustrates the toll meth can take on the human body. The top photograph shows a thirty-six-year-old woman before she started using meth. The bottom photograph shows the same woman four years later, after she had started using and abusing the drug.

MATT'S STORY

Matt was at a party when his friend Freddy gave him a mirror with a line of meth on it. "You only live once," Freddy said, handing him a straw. Matt felt nervous, but he wanted to impress Freddy, so he snorted the powder.

When Freddy asked him how he felt, Matt began talking rapidly, trying to explain the feeling of pleasure that he suddenly felt throughout his body. Freddy also did a line. After a few minutes, they decided that the party was boring, so they left and walked around until the sun came up.

A few months later, Matt found himself snorting meth every weekend. It was cheap, and he could stay up the entire weekend by snorting just a few lines. Freddy's parents were seldom home, and sometimes Matt spent his weekends at his friend's house. The two of them would snort meth and watch movies all day and all night long.

Before Matt tried meth, his weekends were very busy. He would often meet friends for movies or go on short road trips. Now his weekends were always the same: he'd either be alone in his room listening to music high on meth, or he'd be hanging out at Freddy's house high on meth.

One night, as Matt's heart was pounding in his chest from all the meth he'd done, he began to feel faint.

"Freddy, I'm not feeling so good," he said. Matt was having a hard time thinking straight, and Freddy was scared to take Matt to the hospital because he didn't want to get in trouble. Freddy just gave Matt the keys to his car.

Matt tried to pay attention to his driving as sweat poured down his forehead. He was driving erratically, and soon he saw flashing lights in his rearview mirror. Matt thought about trying to outdrive the police car but then decided to play it cool. The policeman wasn't fooled, however, and arrested Matt for driving under the influence. He also called for an ambulance.

When Matt's parents came to the hospital, his mother was crying and his father was trying to comfort her. Matt felt embarrassed and sad to see his parents distraught.

"I'm sorry, Mom," he said, but that just made her cry harder.

"How long has this been going on?" his father asked.

"I don't know. A couple of months, I guess. I'm really sorry."

"He's lucky," a doctor said, coming into the room. "I've seen people die from having the kind of fun you were having, Matt. I'm glad that someone caught you before that happened. Matt needs some rest right now," the doctor said to Matt's parents, "but you should come back tomorrow so we can discuss treatment options. You might have a long road ahead of you, Matt, but things will work out if you try hard."

After seeing how much he had hurt his parents, and that he could have died the previous night, Matt realized the strong hold meth had on his life. He made the promise that he would never use meth again and decided he would seek drug treatment.

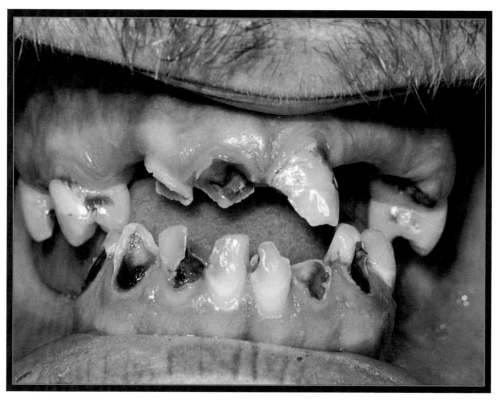

Meth is extraordinarily harmful to the human body. This meth user's teeth have rotted away after years of neglect and meth abuse.

MODELS OF ADDICTION

About 5 percent of the world's population consumed illicit drugs in 2005, according to the United Nations 2005 World Drug Report. Approximately 9.4 percent of the U.S. population age twelve or older had trouble with substance abuse or addiction. Studies have shown that addiction generally affects young people the most, as well as people on the lower end of the socioeconomic spectrum. This doesn't mean, however, that there aren't plenty of people in the middle and upper classes who don't also suffer from substance abuse and addiction.

A user's risk of addiction depends on many physical and psychological factors, including personality, social environment, and peer influences. Some people have brain chemistries that make them more inclined to addiction, and some people are psychologically predisposed to addiction. It's impossible to tell which casual meth user may one day become a meth addict.

No one is quite sure what causes addiction, but there are a number of theories as to why some people seem to be more susceptible to addiction than others. These theories are often called "models."

Moral Model of Addiction

According to the moral model of addiction, addiction is the result of something wrong in the addict's character. People who believe in this model of addiction think there are no biological causes for drug addiction, and that the only reason an addict keeps abusing substances is that he or she doesn't really want to quit. While it might be comfortable for some people to believe that all drug addicts are just weak people who should know better, this model of addiction does not hold much weight in the scientific community.

Genetic Model of Addiction

According to the genetic model of addiction, biological factors can help predict who might be at risk of becoming an addict. For instance, a history of substance abuse in a person's family may be an indicator that that person is vulnerable to addiction. While many experts cite compelling evidence that people can inherit a genetic predisposition to addiction, many also believe that environment plays an important factor along with a genetic predisposition. People born into a family of substance abusers may be more likely to abuse substances themselves—whether or not they are genetically predisposed. Many scientists believe that a combination of genetics and learned behavior makes some people more likely to become addicts.

Disease Model of Addiction

Born out of the twelve-step program of Alcoholics Anonymous, the disease model of addiction views chemical dependency as an illness that can be acute, chronic, or progressive. Much like chronic diseases such as diabetes or heart disease, drug addictions are not curable but are treatable and can be managed through abstinence. Drug addicts must abstain from substances for the rest of their lives if they hope to avoid relapsing into addiction.

Not everyone agrees with the disease model of addiction. For instance, some alcoholics have learned how to drink responsibly after long periods of abstinence. Others have one drink after years of sobriety and completely relapse. Despite the debate over the disease model, it is undeniably effective in treating substance addiction.

WHAT IS A DRUG ADDICT?

People are considered addicts if they keep using a drug even though they know it is harmful. Addicts may also be physically dependent on the drug. This is when the body craves the drug and is unable to function normally without it. Addicts deprived of the substances they are dependent on go through withdrawal, which can often be physically and mentally harrowing.

Withdrawal from meth has less pronounced physical effects than withdrawal from other drugs, but it can still be dangerous. Meth addicts complain that they feel sluggish or mentally slow after giving up the drug. The psychological component of meth addiction is very strong. Coupled with the low cost and wide availability of meth, it can be very difficult for an addict to stop using.

Methamphetamine alters the way the brain handles a chemical called dopamine, which is produced naturally by the body. Dopamine helps determine how the brain controls the body's movements, and it affects the way the brain processes information.

31

A lack of dopamine can interfere with a person's memory and attention span. Parkinson's disease, which causes its sufferers to tremble uncontrollably, is a result of a shortage of dopamine in the brain. Disruption in the release of dopamine has been linked to severe mental illnesses.

Of all the important functions that dopamine performs, one of the most crucial is the way it provides the sensations of pleasure, enjoyment, satisfaction, and motivation. When dopamine is released, the brain is flooded with pleasurable feelings. This is part of the body's natural reward system. Dopamine is released when a person does things like eat, exercise, or fall in love. Pleasure is a powerful motivator; unconsciously, we strive to do things that will cause our bodies to release more dopamine. In this sense, people are "addicted" to the things that will help them stay alive and live a prosperous life.

Meth causes the body to release dopamine, but it also blocks the brain from reabsorbing it. The dopamine stays in the brain longer, resulting in a feeling of euphoria that is very hard to achieve naturally. This means that meth disrupts the body's natural reward system. There are few things drug users could do that would flood their brains with as much dopamine as meth does. The lives of users begin to center around the drug, and addicts start neglecting things that were once important to them. Nothing can provide addicts with the same amount of pleasure as doing drugs. Hanging out with friends, listening to music, and even falling in love pale in comparison to the synthetic rush of meth.

The body can release only a limited amount of dopamine. Although meth users may take more and more of the drug, they will be chemically unable to get the same amount of pleasure from it. Studies show that long-term meth use may impact the ability of a user's brain to keep producing dopamine, and thus can cause brain damage. Some users undergo profound periods of depression and have suicidal thoughts.

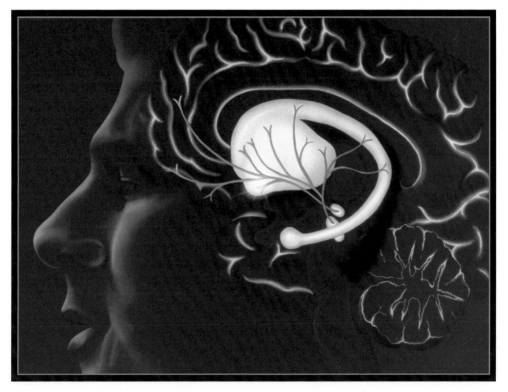

This illustration depicts dopamine being released into the brain. Doctors and scientists are still working to understand the role that dopamine plays in the human body. In the future, this research may help in understanding drug addiction and how to treat and prevent it.

How Can You Tell If Someone You Know Is a Meth User?

There are a few ways to tell if someone you know has been using methamphetamine. People who are high on meth often talk very rapidly and compulsively perform some sort of repetitive action. They may also have dilated pupils and complain of an irregular heartbeat. Other common side effects are nausea, diarrhea, chest pains, and shortness of breath. Users may have scabs on their arms or face from picking at their skin, or may have needle marks on their arms if they inject the drug. Over time, users often begin neglecting personal hygiene and may appear unwashed. Someone on meth may also be extremely paranoid, aggressive, or even violent.

According to the 2004 National Survey on Drug Use and Health, 583,000 Americans age twelve to seventeen had admitted to using meth at least once that year. The number of people being admitted to treatment for amphetamine and methamphetamine abuse rose above 300 percent between 1993 and 2003. In 2003, 57 per 100,000 people age twelve or older entered treatment facilities for these drugs, primarily for methamphetamine in the United States. In states where meth is more widespread, these rates are much higher.

GETTING HELP

A supportive network of friends and family members can make the difference between life and death for an addict. The emotional support of loved ones often helps addicts acknowledge their problem and encourages them to find the strength to stop using drugs.

Rehabilitation facilities across the United States offer treatment for various types of drug addiction. Some patients voluntarily enter drug rehab. Others are ordered to undergo treatment by an employer, school, or court of law. Many drug treatment centers offer family programs. They provide a place where family members can have safe, mediated discussions with the person seeking treatment. These programs also help family members begin to build a new, drug-free life in partnership with their loved ones.

Often, a period of detoxification, or detox, is advised for meth addicts. Detox is a span of time in which a person is monitored while abstaining from drug use. Detox lasts until all traces of the drug leave the user's body.

THERAPY

There is still a lot that researchers don't know about meth's long-term effects on the body and brain. The medical community offers no cure-all drug to free meth users from their addiction. Unlike heroin or cocaine, meth withdrawal does not involve many physical symptoms. The psychological effects of meth withdrawal, however, can be devastating. Antidepressants can be helpful in getting meth users through the tough period after they stop using the drug, but they are not a cure for addiction.

After a thorough detoxification, treatment for methamphetamine use generally involves therapy to help users recognize their problem and break the patterns of their addiction. The sooner a

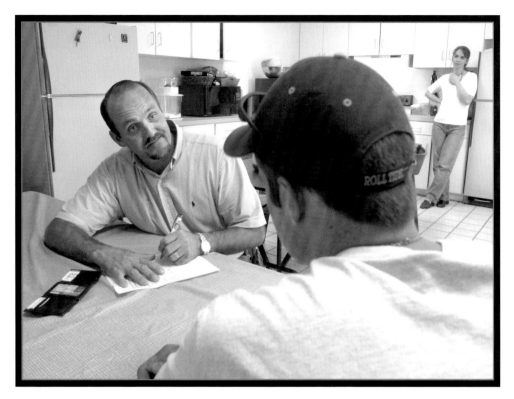

If a person has a meth addiction, there are many ways in which he or she can get help. Todd Sasser *(left)* and his wife, Donna *(far right)*, are reformed meth users who now run Crossroads Ministry in Opp, Alabama. Sasser is enrolling a client into his nineteen-week treatment program in this April 2005 photo.

person recognizes he or she has a drug problem and seeks treatment for it, the easier quitting will be. The more advanced a drug problem is, however, the more difficult it is to overcome. With the help of friends and family members, and a supportive environment, drug users can get their lives back together.

CHAPTER 4
Meth and the Legal System

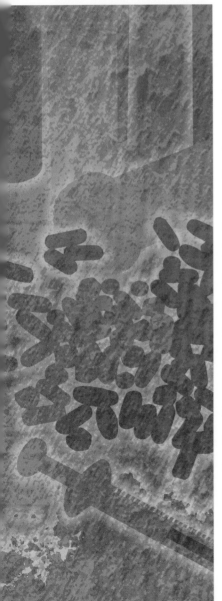

Being on meth increases the likelihood that a person will commit a crime. The link between drugs and crime was illustrated in data collected by the 1998 National Institute of Justice's Arrestee Drug Abuse Monitoring Program. The data ranged from 42.5 percent of male arrestees in Anchorage, Alaska, testing positive for drug use, to nearly 78 percent testing positive in Philadelphia, Pennsylvania. The statistics were more wide-ranging for women: about 33 percent of women arrested in Laredo, Texas, tested positive for drugs, while more than 80 percent of women arrested in New York City tested positive for drugs. The crimes most closely associated with people who abuse drugs are vehicular theft, breaking and entering, and other forms of robbery, as well as prostitution and narcotic sales.

Identity Theft

Identity theft is the illegal acquisition of a victim's personal information, such as a person's Social Security number or credit card information. This crime has become increasingly common among meth addicts. While people steal others' personal information for a number of purposes, one of the most common is credit card fraud. By taking out a fake credit card in someone else's name, a criminal can quickly purchase any number of things and then simply throw the card away.

Some meth addicts turn to identity theft to fund their habit. Often, they steal people's mail and give it to the head of an identity theft ring in exchange for drugs. With the increased energy, concentration, and wakefulness that meth affords its users, people can spend all night stealing mail from mailboxes or even going through people's trash, looking for things such as preapproved credit card applications.

CLASSIFICATION AND LEGISLATION

The Controlled Substances Act (CSA), which is part of the Comprehensive Drug Abuse Prevention and Control Act of 1970, classifies all drugs into one of five categories, known as schedules. The U.S. Drug Enforcement Administration (DEA) sorts drugs into schedules based on their beneficial value for use in medicine, the potential harm they can cause, and how addictive they are.

Methamphetamine is a Schedule II drug. Schedule II drugs are used for medicinal purposes, but also have a high potential for abuse and addiction. Other Schedule II drugs include cocaine, opium, morphine, and barbiturates. The penalties for trafficking (selling on a large scale) Schedule II drugs are very stiff and always involve prison time. If a person is caught trafficking 0.2 to 1.7 ounces (5 to 49 grams) of pure metham-phetamine, or 1.8 to 17.6 ounces (50 to 499 g) of mixed methamphetamine, he or she faces a prison sentence of five to forty years and a fine of up to $2 million. Multiple offenses carry stricter sentences.

Penalties for possession of Schedule II drugs vary by state and region, and may include jail sentences or assignment to a drug rehabilitation clinic. Federal penalties might include a one-year prison sentence and a fine for first-time offenders. The convic-tions could be even steeper for multiple offenders. Generally, rehabilitation is much cheaper than incarceration. According to the U.S. Department of Justice, the average cost of incarcerating a prison inmate was about $23,000 a year in 2001. The National Treatment Improvement Evaluation Study reveals that it cost about $3,000 for a course of treatment in 1995. Meth users and dealers made up about 12 percent of all federal drug arrests from October 1, 2000, to September 30, 2001. During that same time period, 3,932 people were arrested for amphetamines and methamphetamines, and their sentences averaged about eighty-nine months. That's a long time to spend behind bars. Many states have passed even stricter sentencing laws for people who assist in the manufacture of methamphetamine.

DRUG COURT

Introduced in Florida in 1989, drug court is a system in which drug offenders can enter treatment to avoid a prison sentence. Not everyone is considered for drug court. Offenders who are guilty of less serious crimes, like driving under the influence or drug possession, are more likely to be eligible. People who participate in drug court have to plead guilty and enter treatment. They also have to pass regular drug tests. If they successfully complete treatment, the charges against them are dropped. If they don't, however, they go to prison. There are now drug courts in every state.

CONTROLLING INGREDIENTS

Unlike drugs such as cocaine or heroin, which are imported from other countries, meth can be made inside the United States. The proliferation of cheap, simple meth labs means that targeting users alone won't stop the spread of the drug. Instead, recent legislation has been designed to make it more difficult to produce methamphetamine. Because most of the ingredients used in the manufacture of meth are technically legal, there is no way to stop people from acquiring them. However, laws have been passed that make it difficult for people to obtain large amounts of these substances.

The Comprehensive Methamphetamine Control Act (MCA) of 1996 placed restrictions on the purchase of chemicals used to make meth. It also increased the maximum legal penalties for manufacturing the drug. The Methamphetamine Anti-Proliferation Act (MAPA) was passed as part of the Children's Health Act of 2000. Once again, it increased penalties for the possession or sale of meth. It also created a budget for training law enforcement officers to investigate methamphetamine manufacturing and seize meth labs.

There are a number of different ways to manufacture meth. This lab is set up to make meth using the Birch reduction method. This method is very popular among manufacturers because it yields fairly pure meth, requires little chemistry knowledge, has a short production time, and the lab can be easily moved.

A number of states have passed laws restricting the amount of ephedrine or pseudoephedrine that a person can purchase. Oregon has been particularly aggressive in this regard. In April 2005, the state required people to sign a registry when buying over-the-counter cold medicines containing pseudoephedrine. This way, the police know who has been buying products containing pseudoephedrine and how much that person has been buying. This law forces potential meth cooks to travel across the state border if they want to get supplies. The law has substantially reduced the state's illegal meth activity. In 2004, Oregon law enforcement agents seized 447 meth labs. In 2005, after the law went into effect, they seized only 185 labs, a reduction of nearly 60 percent.

Though it is hard to argue with the law's effectiveness, it has not entirely stopped the meth problem in Oregon. Some meth cooks travel out of state to buy pseudoephedrine. A number of them hop from pharmacy to pharmacy and purchase the minimum amount of pseudoephedrine they can without being recorded on the registry. This practice is known as "smurfing," and allows meth cooks to operate in a somewhat limited manner despite restrictions. While meth is still prevalent in Oregon, it is now much more difficult to manufacture it there.

METH IN THE PATRIOT ACT

After the terrorist attacks of September 11, 2001, on the World Trade Center in New York City and the Pentagon outside of

Washington, D.C., Congress passed the Patriot Act. The goal of the act is to make it easier for intelligence agencies and law enforcement agents to prevent terrorist attacks on U.S. soil. It is a controversial piece of legislation: many feel it restricts people's civil liberties.

More provisions have been added to the Patriot Act, including a package of anti-methamphetamine measures in 2005. This package of legislation is called the Combat Meth Act, and it is the most aggressive meth bill ever put in front of Congress. It requires states to place medicines with pseudoephedrine behind pharmacy counters. It also limits the amount of medicine containing pseudoephedrine a person can purchase and forces people to sign a logbook so their purchases can be tracked. Many large retail chains such as Wal-Mart and Walgreens have already chosen to limit the sale of cold products, but this new legislation, if passed, would make such restrictions mandatory.

The Combat Meth Act will place further restrictions on the sale of meth ingredients and will give police additional tools in the fight against the drug if it is passed. It will also allocate extra money to help meth addicts recover from their addiction.

PSEUDOEPHEDRINE IN MEXICO

Much of the meth in the United States comes from Mexico, where pseudoephedrine is easier to acquire. With more and more Mexican superlabs being raided, the Mexican government

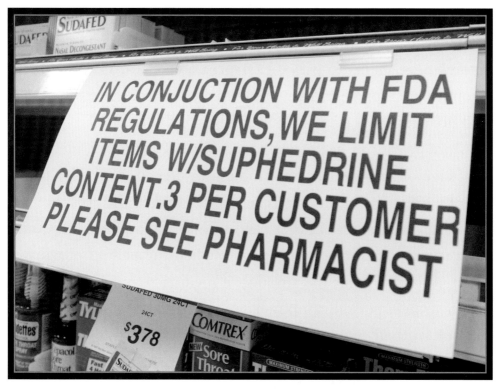

Signs like this one, in a store in Columbus, Indiana, are becoming more common. Many laws are being passed that restrict the sale of over-the-counter medications containing pseudoephedrine. The medications are kept behind the counter, and customers are limited to the amount that they can buy.

began passing restrictions on how much pseudoephedrine can be imported into the country. In 2004, Mexico imported about 224 tons (203 metric tons) of pseudoephedrine. In 2005, only 134 tons (122 metric tons) of the chemical were imported. Mexico also passed legislation to make sure that medications containing pseudoephedrine can only be acquired by pharmacies and must be kept behind the counter.

CHAPTER 5

Meth and Society

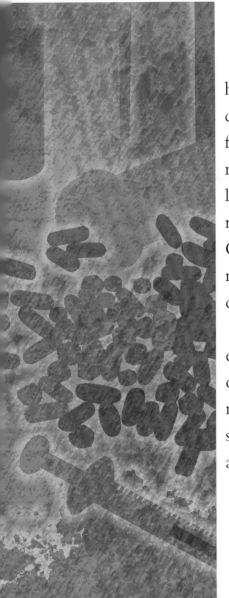

Meth has a devastating impact on individuals, families, and entire communities. Once meth has its hooks in a user, it doesn't want to let go. It can take years for an addict to recover fully from meth use. During this time, he or she may feel fuzzy-headed and unsatisfied with life, since the brain's centers of pleasure and reward have been altered by the drug. Once meth gets a foothold in a community, it can be economically and socially catastrophic.

Cleaning up meth labs, providing law enforcement agents with training, imprisoning dealers, providing treatment for meth addicts, and putting the children of some meth addicts into protective services all cost money. Some of this money can be recovered by fining meth lab operators. However, taxpayers end up bearing the bulk of the burden.

METH AND THE FAMILY

A side effect of meth use is extreme aggression. Often, the targets of this aggression are the people closest to the addicts. In some areas of California where meth is particularly prevalent, the

Dressed in a protective suit, Sergeant Thomas Mahoney leads a demonstration on methamphetamine in Dunlap, Tennessee, in March 2003. Meth task forces use a lot of specialized equipment, like the detection kit that Mahoney is holding.

majority of domestic violence cases that police investigated involved meth use.

The children of many meth addicts are abused and neglected. There are countless stories of law enforcement agents raiding a home that contains a meth lab and finding children living in extremely squalid conditions. The process of cooking meth can leave residue on surfaces all over the home, exposing all of its occupants to the drug. Chemicals that need to be kept cold are often stored in the refrigerator, where they can contaminate food. Often, children who live in meth labs are extremely mal-nourished.

A THREAT TO THE UNBORN

Just like any other harmful substance, meth can pose a threat to unborn children. However, there is not enough data for researchers to come to any solid conclusions about the effects of meth on children in the womb. Still, anecdotal evidence has revealed some startling facts. Some babies are born prematurely to mothers who are using meth. Even those who are carried to full term exhibit a number of the same behaviors and symptoms as premature babies. For instance, they may have trouble swallow-ing and are often very sensitive to touch.

Although none of the children studied appeared to be men-tally disabled when they grew older, there is a chance that unborn children may suffer strokes while in the womb. Meth constricts blood vessels in a user's body. When a pregnant woman uses the drug, it can also constrict the blood vessels of the placenta, the organ that nourishes an unborn baby. This can affect the fetus's heart rate and its growth. Although some deformities have been observed in fetuses exposed to methamphetamine, there has not been any definitive evidence linking the two.

SMALL-TIME METH LABS

One reason that meth production is thriving despite the efforts of drug enforcement agents is that the drug is so easy to manufacture. A garage, trailer, or even a rented storage space can serve as a meth lab. When an illegal lab is busted by the police, another one can quickly spring up in its place.

There is no surefire way for drug enforcement agents to determine the location of a meth lab. There are some signs that homes may contain labs, such as extensive security, large amounts of trash outside, and unusual chemical odors coming from inside. Another sign that a home may contain a meth lab is that its occupants always go outside when smoking cigarettes, sometimes standing a good distance away from their home so as not to ignite the flammable chemicals inside the laboratory.

People who operate small, clandestine labs are not as well organized as large drug cartels. Generally, the cooks at small meth labs aren't highly skilled, and it's common for them to be on drugs while manufacturing the meth. This can seriously impair their judgment, leading to accidents and fires. Sometimes, children are found living in meth labs, neglected and seriously ill from the chemicals in the air. Superlabs produce most of the meth and are thus a bigger priority for law enforcement. However, small labs account for many more fires and explosions, and therefore present their own challenges and dangers to the community.

SEIZING METH LABS

When meth labs are raided, drug enforcement agents wear respirators and hazardous materials (hazmat) suits as they confiscate the illegal materials inside. For each pound (0.5 kg) of

This Arizona family stands reunited in August 2005. The state took Linda Galloway and Scott Shepherd's daughter, Amanda, away from them because of the couple's addiction to meth. Both parents worked hard to rehabilitate themselves and eventually got their daughter back.

meth a lab produces, it also produces about 5 to 7 pounds (2.3–3.2 kg) of toxic waste. This waste is extremely dangerous, and there is no legal way for a person running a meth lab to dispose of it. As a result, the toxic waste from meth production is often poured down storm drains, into rivers, or just dumped on the ground. These chemicals are major pollutants and are often flammable, explosive, and corrosive. They are hazardous to the health of not only the person dumping them, but also to the people in the surrounding community. The waste left over from cooking a batch of meth can easily leak into the groundwater, sometimes harming people who don't even live near the lab.

If the meth lab is still in operation, it must first be "neutralized." This means that police subdue and arrest anyone on the premises, and make sure there is no danger of the meth lab exploding. After the lab has been neutralized, any clearly toxic chemicals are safely disposed of. The chemicals remaining in the lab are then tested to determine how dangerous they are. It costs law enforcement officers up to $10,000 to clean up a small-scale meth lab. A superlab can cost upward of $150,000 to clean up. In 2004, approximately 9,300 meth labs were seized in the United States, more than five times the number seized in 1996. The DEA budget for cleaning up clandestine drug laboratories increased from $2 million in 1995 to $16.2 million in 2003. In 2004, the DEA spent $17.8 million on cleaning up meth labs.

CHAPTER 6
Meth and the Media

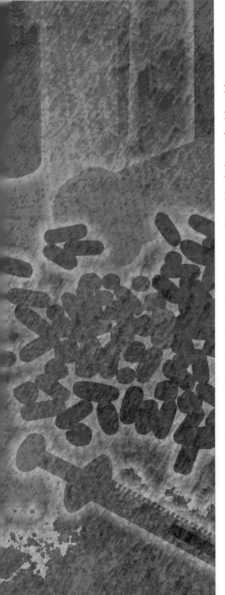

The American media devote a lot of time to covering meth use in America. Much of this coverage is very dramatic. Indeed, the effects of meth on people and communities can be extremely frightening. However, some people have questioned whether the media present the meth epidemic accurately.

A common media misconception is that meth mouth is caused by the toxic chemicals used to manufacture methamphetamine. Many articles point to the fact that meth is made from a number of acidic substances and claim that smoking the drug corrodes the user's teeth. The truth is that meth mouth is caused by users grinding their teeth and the poor dental hygiene of many addicts. Also, meth causes the mouth to

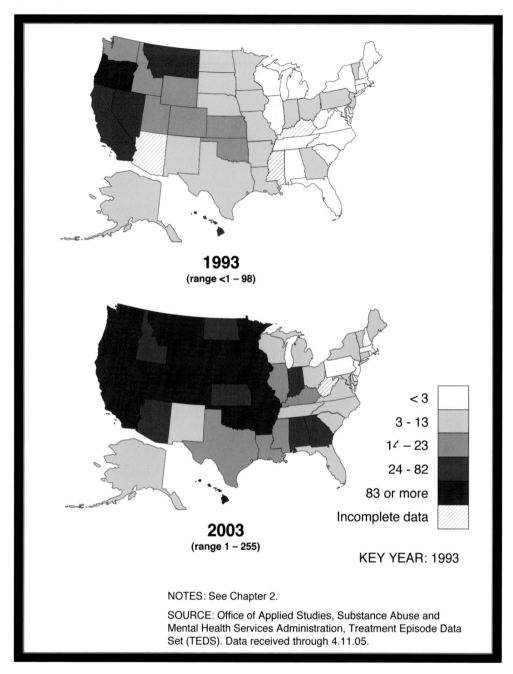

1993
(range <1 – 98)

2003
(range 1 – 255)

< 3

3 - 13

1⁄ – 23

24 - 82

83 or more

Incomplete data

KEY YEAR: 1993

NOTES: See Chapter 2.

SOURCE: Office of Applied Studies, Substance Abuse and
Mental Health Services Administration, Treatment Episode Data
Set (TEDS). Data received through 4.11.05.

These maps show the dramatic increase in people who entered methamphetamine treatment and indicate how quickly the drug has spread across
the United States over a ten-year period. The key at the right shows how
many people, age twelve or older, per 100,000 were admitted to meth treatment. From 1993 to 2003, the enrollment rate of those seeking meth
treatment jumped 307 percent in the United States.

produce less saliva than normal, depriving users of the natural enzymes that help prevent tooth decay.

The damage that meth does to unborn children has also been misrepresented in the media. While pregnant women should certainly not be using drugs, and virtually every drug can harm an unborn child, no study has provided conclusive

Ten Facts About Methamphetamine

- About 5 percent of the world's population consumed illicit drugs in 2005, according to the United Nations 2005 World Drug Report.
- In 2003, 57 people per 100,000 age twelve or older in the United States admitted themselves into drug treatment, primarily for methamphetamine abuse.
- According to the 2004 National Survey on Drug Use and Health, 583,000 Americans age twelve to seventeen had confessed to using methamphetamine at least once that year.
- The number of people admitted to treatment for amphetamine and methamphetamine abuse in the United States rose more than 300 percent between 1993 and 2003.
- Meth is one of the most addictive illegal drugs in the world.
- No medical drug treatments have proven to be effective in treating meth addiction.
- It costs law enforcement officers up to $10,000 to clean up a small-scale meth lab.
- It costs law enforcement officers up to $150,000 to clean up a superlab.
- In 2004, the DEA spent $17.8 million on cleaning up meth labs.
- It costs less money to treat a person for meth use than to imprison the abuser.

evidence of meth's effect on a fetus's development. While babies born to meth users have a higher incidence of birth defects, pregnant women who use meth are also more likely to use other drugs, drink alcohol, and smoke cigarettes—all of which can harm an unborn child. It is not clear if it's solely meth that causes the defects.

Although it's clear that meth has grown more popular, some statistics show that its use leveled out between the years 2002 and 2003. It's difficult to say for sure, as it may be impossible to calculate accurately the national incidence of methamphetamine use. A July 2004 report from the Drug Abuse Warning Network showed that emergency room admissions for methamphetamine have doubled from 1995 to 2002, but the increase has not necessarily been a steady one. Some data point to the fact that emergency room admissions have dropped when measures have been taken to restrict the sale of pseudoephedrine.

There is no denying that meth is an extremely dangerous and addictive drug. Wherever it spreads, it leaves devastation in its wake. With any luck, legislation will limit meth's availability. Meanwhile, scientists and doctors are learning more about this dangerous drug. In the future, there may be more effective ways to treat meth addiction. Education can help people make the right choices. The more people know about meth, the more likely they will be to avoid it.

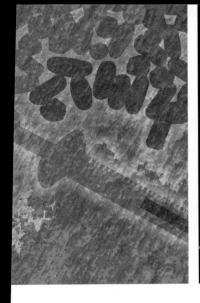

GLOSSARY

amphetamine A stimulant drug first synthesized in the nineteenth century.

Benzedrine One of the first commercially released forms of amphetamine. Benzedrine was intended to be used as a decongestant and came in an inhaler.

black market An underground marketplace where illegal goods are sold and purchased.

cocaine An illegal stimulant with effects somewhat resembling those of methamphetamine.

dopamine An important natural chemical that, among other things, causes a person to feel pleasure, enjoyment, and satisfaction.

euphoria An intense feeling of pleasure.

hepatitis C A disease that attacks the liver.

human immunodeficiency virus (HIV) A virus that destroys the immune system and causes acquired immunodeficiency syndrome (AIDS).

insomnia The inability to sleep.

meth mouth The extensive tooth decay that most meth users experience.

paranoia A psychological condition in which a person believes that everyone is out to harm him or her.

tolerance A body's resistance to a drug's effects.

tweaking When a meth user desperately tries to achieve the same rush that he or she experienced when first doing the drug, but without any success.

withdrawal The often unpleasant, and sometimes deadly, physical symptoms that an addict goes through after abstaining from particular drugs.

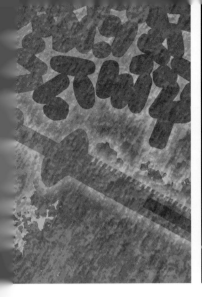

Families Anonymous, Inc.
P.O. Box 3475
Culver City, CA 90231–3475
(800) 736-9805
Web site: http://
   www.familiesanonymous.org

Nar-Anon Family Group
Headquarters, Inc.
22527 Crenshaw Blvd., #200B
Torrance, CA 90505
(800) 477-6291
Web site: http://nar-anon.org/
   index.html

Narcotics Anonymous
World Service Office in
   Los Angeles

P.O. Box 9999
Van Nuys, CA 91409
(818) 773-9999
Web site: http://www.na.org

WEB SITES

Due to the changing nature
of Internet links, Rosen
Publishing has developed an
online list of Web sites related
to the subject of this book.
This site is updated regularly.
Please use this link to access
the list:

http://www.rosenlinks.com/
   das/meth

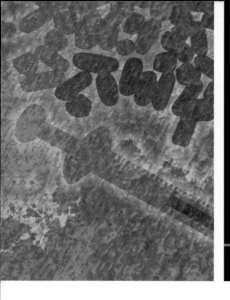

FOR FURTHER READING

Bayer, Linda N. *Amphetamines and Other Uppers.* New York, NY: Chelsea House Publications, 1999.

Clayton, Lawrence. *Amphetamines and Other Stimulants.* New York, NY: Rosen Publishing, 2001.

Cobb, Allan B. *Speed and Your Brain: The Incredibly Disgusting Story.* New York, NY: Rosen Publishing, 2003.

Herscovitch, Arthur G. *Everything You Need to Know About Drug Abuse.* New York, NY: Rosen Publishing, 1999.

Marcovitz, Hal. *Methamphetamine.* San Diego, CA: Lucent Books, 2005.

Marshall, Shelly. *Young, Sober & Free.* Center City, MN: Hazelden Publishing, 2003.

Nagle, Jeanne. *Everything You Need to Know About Drug Addiction.* New York, NY: Rosen Publishing, 1999.

Shuker-Haines, Frances. *Everything You Need to Know About a Drug-Abusing Parent.* New York, NY: Rosen Publishing, 1997.

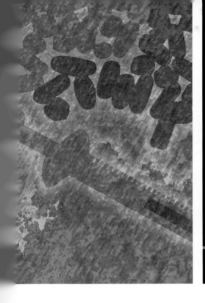

BIBLIOGRAPHY

Associated Press. "Cold-Remedy Registry Cuts Meth Trade, Oregon Authorities Say." *Seattle Post-Intelligencer,* January 6, 2006. Retrieved January 15, 2006 (http://seattlepi.nwsource.com/local/254953_methoregon09.html).

Benson, Rodney G. "Stopping the Methamphetamine Epidemic: Lessons from the Pacific Northwest." U.S. Drug Enforcement Administration Congressional Testimony. Retrieved February 28, 2006 (http://www.dea.gov/pubs/cngrtest/ct101405.html).

Drug Abuse Warning Network. "Amphetamine and Methamphetamine Emergency Department Visits, 1995–2002." *The Dawn Report,* July 2004. Retrieved February 28, 2006 (http://dawninfo.samhsa.gov/old_dawn/pubs_94_02/shortreports/files/DAWN_tdr_amphetamine.pdf).

Eschliman, Bob. "Methamphetamine: The Plague." *Le Mars Daily Sentinel,* December 20, 2005. Retrieved January 15, 2006 (http://www.lemarssentinel.com/story/1132131.html).

Heredia, Christopher. "Dance of Death: Crystal Meth Fuels HIV." *San Francisco Chronicle,* May 4, 2004. Retrieved May 17,

2006 (http://www.sfgate.com/cgi-bin/article.cgi?file=/chronicle/archive/2003/05/04/MN281636.DTL).

Lewis, David C. "Meth Science Not Stigma: Open Letter to the Media." *Join Together*, July 25, 2005. Retrieved January 8, 2006 (http://www.jointogether.org/sa/news/features/reader/0,1854,577769,00.html).

Lloyd, Jennifer. "Methamphetamine." ONDCP Drug Policy Information Clearinghouse Fact Sheet, November 2003. Retrieved January 15, 2006 (http://www.whitehousedrugpolicy.org/publications/factsht/methamph/index.html).

McLellan, A. Thomas, David C. Lewis, Charles P. O'Brien, and Herbert D. Kleber. "Drug Dependence, a Chronic Medical Illness: Implications for Treatment, Insurance, and Outcomes Evaluation." *Journal of American Medicine Association*, Vol. 284, No. 13, October 4, 2000. Retrieved January 8, 2006 (http://www.tresearch.org/resources/pubs/09_McLellan_JAMA.pdf).

Mills, Kimberly. "Meth of Old Has Morphed Into Epidemic Proportions." *Seattle Post-Intelligencer*, December 13, 1999. Retrieved February 28, 2002 (http://seattlepi.nwsource.com/methamphetamines/drug.shtml).

Milne, David. "Experts Desperately Seeking Meth Abuse Prevention, Treatment." *Psychiatric News*, Vol. 38, No. 1, January 3, 2003. Retrieved January 15, 2006 (http://pn.psychiatryonline.org/cgi/content/full/psychnews;38/1/12).

National Drug Intelligence Center. "National Drug Threat Assessment 2005." February 2005. Retrieved February 28,

2006 (http://www.usdoj.gov/ndic/pubs11/12620/
meth.htm#Top).

Office of National Drug Control Policy. "Methamphetamine."
Drug Facts. Retrieved January 15, 2006 (http://
www.whitehousedrugpolicy.gov/drugfact/methamphetamine/
index.html).

Rodgers, Joann Ellison. "Addiction—A Whole New View."
Psychology Today, September/October 1994. Retrieved
January 15, 2006 (http://www.psychologytoday.com/articles/
pto-19940901-000020.html).

Rother, Caitlin. "Toxic Environment: While Grown-Ups Cook
Meth, Children Are Put in Danger." *San Diego Union-Tribune*,
October 16, 2005. Retrieved January 2006 (http://
www.signonsandiego.com/uniontrib/20051016/news_
lz1c16toxic.html).

Sanchez, Devonne R., and Blake Harrison. "The Methamphetamine Menace." National Conference of State Legislatures
Legisbrief, Vol. 12, No. 1, January 2004. Retrieved January 15,
2006 (http://www.ncsl.org/programs/cj/meth.pdf).

Scott, Michael S. "Clandestine Drug Labs." U.S. Department of
Justice. Retrieved January 15, 2006 (http://www.cops.usdoj.gov/
mime/open.pdf?Item=274).

Seper, Jerry. "Patriot Act Report Targets Meth." *Washington
Times*, December 12, 2005. Retrieved January 15, 2006
(http://www.washtimes.com/national/20051211-
110231-2800r.htm).

Suo, Steve, and Erin Hoover Barnett. "Special Investigative Report: Unnecessary Epidemic: A Five-Part Series." *Oregonian*, October 3–7, 2004. Retrieved January 15, 2006 (http://www.oregonlive.com/special/oregonian/meth).

U.S. Department of Health and Human Services. "Nation's Youth Turning Away from Marijuana, as Perceptions of Risk Rise; Most Adults with Substance Abuse Problems Are Employed." September 9, 2004. Retrieved January 15, 2006 (http://www.hhs.gov/news/press/2004pres/20040909b.html).

U.S. Department of Justice. "Drugs and Crime Facts." October 24, 2005. Retrieved February 28, 2006 (http://www.ojp.usdoj.gov/bjs/dcf/duc.htm).

Weissert, Will. "To Fight Meth, Mexico Cracks Down on Cold-Pill Ingredient." *San Diego Union-Tribune*, November 27, 2005. Retrieved January 15, 2006 (http://www.signonsandiego.com/uniontrib/20051127/news_1n27mexmeth.html).

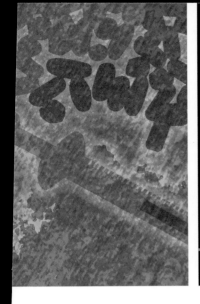

INDEX

2

ABOUT THE AUTHOR

Frank Spalding is a writer living in New York state. In the process of researching and writing this book, he developed a great amount of respect and admiration for those who overcome drug addiction.

PHOTO CREDITS

p. 5 photo courtesy of the Drug Enforcement Administration; p. 8 © Custom Medical Stock Photo; p. 11 © Getty Images; pp. 17, 21, 41 FBI Houston HIDTA Methamphetamine Initiative Group (MIG); pp. 23, 36, 44, 46, 49 © AP/Wide World Photos; p. 26 © Handout/Reuters/Corbis: p. 28 courtesy Christopher Heringlake, D.D.S.; p. 33 © Bryson/Custom Medical Stock Photo; p. 52 maps courtesy of the Office of Applied Studies, Substance Abuse and Mental Health Services Administration.

Designer: Tahara Anderson; Editor: Jun Lim; Photo Researcher: Jeffrey Wendt